Should There Be Presidential Term Limits?

Caroline Leavitt

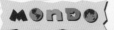

Contents

Introduction

What are term limits and why should we do away with them?

Term limits refers to the amount of time that an elected United States government official can legally serve in a particular office. For example, the president of the United States is allowed to serve for two four-year terms. Then, at the end of the second term, even if the president is doing a great job running the country and is loved by the American people, new presidential candidates are nominated. A president cannot run for a third term. This is the law. But is it a good law?

The leaders who were responsible for establishing our country's government and its laws believed in democracy. In a democracy, we the people—the country's citizens—have the right to vote for whomever we want. The election of the president is in our hands. In our country's early days, there was no such thing as term limits; presidents could run for reelection as many times as they wanted. However, the United States' very first president, George Washington, stepped down from the presidency after serving two terms. He wasn't voted out; he just decided that he wanted to be a private citizen once again. He felt that growing older made it hard for him to perform the duties that his office required.

Thomas Jefferson, the United States' third president, suggested setting a two-term limit for the office of president. However, it's important to remember that times were very different then. America had only recently won independence from England, a country with an all-powerful leader—a king—who served for life. United States citizens didn't want their new country's government to be anything like England's monarchy, where kings or queens often ruled for decades. Jefferson feared that if limits weren't placed on the amount of time a president could serve,

Thomas Jefferson

5

a situation could arise in which we had a president for life—who would be just like a king. It is easy to see how, more than 200 years ago, the idea of presidential term limits would have been appealing. Our country's government was not yet fully formed, so the fear of having a kinglike ruler was a very real one. However, more than two centuries later, isn't it time to reexamine what kind of government would be best for our nation now?

Because our country's early presidents set an example of serving for only two terms, that's the way things remained until 1940. At that time, allies of the United States were fighting in World War II, and instead of turning over the presidency to a new candidate who lacked wartime experience, Democratic president Franklin Roosevelt decided to run for a third term. He was reelected. Four years later, Roosevelt, who was still popular with the people, ran for and won a fourth term. Members of the opposing Republican party began to worry that a Republican president might never again sit in the White House. Others, too, became concerned about the possibility that in the future a president they didn't like could remain in office for decades—even for life! To prevent this from happening, Congress proposed that an amendment, or addition, be made to the United States Constitution (the supreme law of our country) limiting the amount

President Roosevelt being inaugurated for a fourth term in 1945

of time a person could serve as president. The amendment (called the Twenty-Second Amendment) states that a president cannot be elected for more than two four-year terms.

But let's think about this law. If a president is only allowed to be elected to serve for a total of eight years, is this really democratic? After all, aren't the people supposed to be the ones who decide who becomes president? And if the people want a certain person to remain as president past the two-term limit, shouldn't it be their right to make this happen? With term limits, power is taken out of the hands of the people. If voters don't want a particular president, they should have the power to vote that president out of office. The decision shouldn't be made for them in the form of term limits.

Presidents Bill Clinton, Ronald Reagan, and George W. Bush believed that term limits should be changed. Our government is supposed to be for and by the people. That means if we want to elect a president for 5 or even 10 terms, we should have that right.

But let's take a closer look at the issues and investigate why doing away with term limits is really a good idea.

Originally, the Constitution did not include any provisions for presidential term limits.

Being president is a difficult job. To be good at it, a person needs experience.

Think about your favorite professional sports team or a team you play on yourself. Who would you prefer to have on your team: someone with lots of experience playing that sport or someone completely new to the game? Most people who are good at what they do—for example, athletes, musicians, and artists—got that way through many years of practice and learning. It's the same with politicians. It takes time for politicians to learn the ways of government and figure out how to get things done quickly and efficiently. With term limits in place, a president has only two full terms in which to learn the ins and outs of the job and how to do it well. Being president might be the most challenging job in our country. After all, it's the United States' highest government office. Shouldn't the president be given more time to become an expert at the job?

Sports teams count on experienced athletes—like Derek Jeter (top)—to give them a winning edge.

The fact that we have presidential term limits suggests that Americans place less importance on having an experienced president in office than on having a new face in the position every four or eight years. Being president of the United States is perhaps the most difficult job in the world, so of course it requires having an experienced person in the position. Presidents have to master the skills necessary to successfully run the country and deal with foreign affairs the same way that a musician needs to master the guitar or a baseball player needs to master playing shortstop. Sure, pure talent helps, but it can't make up for a lack of experience. Experienced politicians are the ones with the knowledge about what has worked and not worked in the past, and how best to work with the members of Congress and other politicians and world leaders to get things done.

Argument Two

If presidents know their time will not be cut short by term limits, they can better use that time to get things done.

It takes time for presidents not only to gain experience but also to establish policies and accomplish things that are good for the country. Because of term limits, even excellent presidents have only eight years to accomplish everything that they promised during the campaign. Also, in the last couple of years of the second term, the next election campaign begins, and the president becomes what is called a "lame duck." A lame-duck president is less able to get things done, because other politicians, such as members of Congress who are responsible for either approving or rejecting the president's programs, know that there's a good chance the new president might work to reverse the decision anyway. What's the point of going out on a limb to support a president who will soon be out of office?

With a lame-duck president, power begins to shift to other politicians who might or might not support the president's projects, depending on who they suppose the next president will be. Most politicians prefer to get on the good side of the frontrunner in the race to become the next president rather than support the current lame duck. As a result, lame-duck presidents don't have as much motivation to work hard. They have no chance of being reelected, so why bother? But if there weren't term limits, the president would have hopes of winning the next election, spurring him or her on to accomplish great things. No more lame ducks.

Newly elected President George W. Bush is congratulated by President Bill Clinton and Vice-President Al Gore.

The policies a president puts into place often require time and attention in order to work well. A new president isn't likely to provide either one.

When President Franklin D. Roosevelt came into office in 1933, the country was suffering through the Great Depression that began in 1929 when the stock market crashed and banks failed. The depression resulted in many Americans losing their jobs and all of their money. It was a dark, difficult time, and the country was in disorder. In response to the depression, President Roosevelt established a far-reaching set of programs and policies called the New Deal. Among other things, the New Deal was meant to help people get back on their feet by creating new jobs, such as road building and sign painting. With this work, entire families who were penniless and struggling to stay alive were able to patch their lives together again.

This political cartoon shows President Roosevelt leading the American people toward economic recovery.

As noted before, presidential terms limits weren't yet in place, and the American people were able to elect President Roosevelt, whom they trusted and respected, to four terms in office. Now imagine what might have happened to all the people suffering through the depression if President Roosevelt hadn't been able to be reelected so many times. He might not have been in office long enough to see to it that his New Deal programs were running properly. A project as large and complex as the New Deal requires close attention and adjustment over the years in order to succeed. If a new president had been elected instead of Roosevelt, the new leader might not have been capable of ensuring that New Deal programs were successful or might not have been willing to do so.

If we didn't have term limits, popular presidents with good ideas could continue to serve for the length of time necessary to get their programs established. If the policies that a president puts into place are popular with voters, then the president should be allowed to remain in office long enough to ensure that the policies are working well enough to help the people they were intended to help.

Argument Four

In times of crisis, the American people want a president—and an administration— experienced in dealing with such difficulties.

When President Roosevelt was running for his third term, many countries were fighting in World War II. The major reason President Roosevelt was reelected for a third (and then a fourth) term was most likely because the American people wanted their leader to be experienced in governing during wartime. This may be a large part of why George W. Bush won a second term. The country was at war with Iraq at the time of the election, and people might not have been confident that a president without White House and wartime experience could govern as effectively. However, when a president is reelected, it's usually not just about keeping a president with experience in office, but it is also about keeping the other experienced government leaders who serve in the president's administration.

President Bush welcoming soldiers home from Iraq

Every time there's a new president, many other government employees are replaced as well. These new people need time to learn their jobs. The idea of wasting time waiting for people to get up to speed while war is raging and soldiers are dying seems ridiculous. It makes much more sense to keep in office the people who have been dealing with the crisis so far. Think about your class in school, and about how things change when a substitute teacher comes in for a long period of time, say a month. Because the new teacher may not know how the school (or your classroom) runs, it could take a while to learn everything he or she needs to know. Now imagine if there were a crisis in your school, like a fire. A new teacher might not have been in the building long enough to have gone through a fire drill and might not know the best way to get you and your classmates out of the building quickly. This could be dangerous. During such an event, wouldn't you prefer to have your regular teacher there who knows how your school runs and what to do in an emergency?

Not having term limits would allow voters to reelect, in times of crisis or hardship, a president who they feel has the experience necessary to lead the country through troubled times.

Argument Five

Many former presidents believe that past presidents should be allowed to run for office again after their initial terms end.

Former president Bill Clinton believes a past president should be able to run again for the top office after a period of time has passed. He feels this could be especially important during a time of crisis that might have situations the former president has experience dealing with. Former president Ronald Reagan agreed. Suppose, for example, the country had been suffering from a severe economic crisis, and the current president hadn't been able to turn things around. Now imagine that a former president had dealt successfully with a similar situation and had led the country out of trouble. If this past president wanted to run again, don't you think it would be wise to let the voters elect that person? With term limits in place, this couldn't happen.

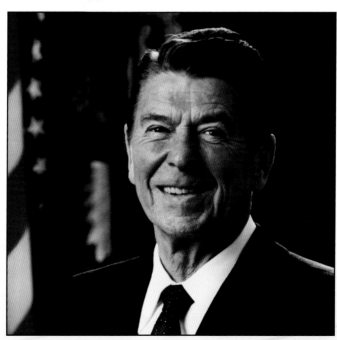

President Reagan was known for his ability
to deal with world leaders.

Argument Six

Many people believe that without term limits, presidents are more likely to fill important government positions with friends who aren't qualified. But this isn't the case.

Cronyism—the placing of friends in positions of power—is usually bad for the country because often these friends aren't well qualified for the job, and their lack of ability may cause problems. People who are for term limits argue that the longer a president is in office, the more time he or she will have to fill important positions with unqualified friends. They also argue that the president's friends are more likely to do what the president wants even if it isn't the best thing for the country. However, cronyism tends to exist even with term limits in place. Most past presidents have given important government jobs to friends, even though these presidents were limited to eight years in office.

Furthermore, it isn't necessarily true that cronyism is bad. Many past presidents have placed friends in important government positions with great success. For example, in 1965, President Lyndon Johnson appointed lawyer Abe Fortas, who had helped him become a United States senator years earlier, to the Supreme Court. Many people thought this was unfair and did not expect much from Fortas, but he wrote many important opinions. Earlier, in 1963, Fortas had argued an important case before the Supreme Court. Until that time, a person who had been charged with a serious crime and couldn't afford

Suprime Court Justice Abe Fortas was a friend of President Lyndon Johnson.

a lawyer often wasn't provided one. Without a lawyer, it was difficult for such a person to prove his or her innocence and to receive justice. Fortas argued that every person has the right to be provided with a lawyer when charged with a serious crime, even if the person can't pay for it. Fortas won a unanimous decision from the court, and now any person charged with a serious crime has the right to free legal counsel if he or she can't afford it.

It's important to remember that a president's friends aren't necessarily unqualified for government positions. Presidents are often friends with other politicians, many of whom are talented, intelligent, and qualified. Even if a president's friends aren't experienced government insiders, that doesn't mean they won't perform well at their new jobs. In fact, sometimes an outsider brings a new, fresh approach to a job and becomes extremely successful. After all, no president wants to be remembered for appointing several failures in government offices. And just because these people are the president's friends, it doesn't mean they'll do only what the president wants and not think for themselves. You and your friends probably like a lot of the same things, but does that mean you always do what your friends tell you? No, you have a mind of your own, just as a president's friends do.

Argument Seven

Every time a new president is elected, many other government workers change as well. This can result in good policies being quickly overturned.

There are two sides to most issues. A president may propose a new law or have a plan that supports one side of an issue. If the next president is from the opposing political party, he or she often works to overturn these policies. This happens even when many Americans support the original plan or policy. For example, when Bill Clinton was president, he promoted many laws designed to protect the environment. Many of the policies President Clinton set up required certain industries to release less pollution and make other expensive changes to the way they did things. Then, when George W. Bush became president, he reversed some of President Clinton's policies that he believed would harm the American economy. Bush was able to do this because, when he came into office, Bush replaced many heads of government agencies with people who believed as he did and would carry out his policies.

If President Clinton had been elected to a third term, his environmental policies would likely have survived longer. And the longer a policy exists, the less likely it is to be overturned, because people come to view it as something they can't live without. Limiting the number of years a president can serve results in good policies being overturned. Shouldn't the American people be responsible for deciding whether or not they approve of a president's policies and want to keep the president in office? After all, if a president's policies are truly unpopular, he or she won't be reelected.

Vice-President Gore and President Clinton at an environmental conference

Rapid presidential turnover can result in a government run by newcomers with little or no experience.

People already serving in government offices may not have the time to take newcomers under their wings or help them figure out how things work. Newcomers' inexperience can be harmful. At first, new government employees might not be able to make their way through the bureaucracy, making it difficult for them to do their jobs. An inexperienced worker brought in by a newly elected president might not know how to deal with pressure from special-interest groups or how to form alliances with the people who can help get an important project working. Lack of experience could result in a new employee's being ineffective and not getting much done. After all, more than 400 people work in the White House, and this doesn't even include house or military staff or members of Congress. Upon starting a government job, it would be impossible for a newcomer to know what all these people do and which of them are most likely to be helpful. So instead of being able to dive into the job, valuable time would be spent learning the ropes.

A thoughtful Jimmy Carter at the start of his presidential term in January 1977

Argument Nine

Term limits cut short the careers of brilliant presidents.

People who are for term limits argue that limiting the number of years presidents can serve prevents bad leaders from remaining in office and doing more harm. However, in a free country, it's supposed to be the people who make the decision about how long a president should remain in office. Do the pro-term-limits people really think voters would reelect bad presidents again and again? If presidents are reelected, it's because the voters think they are doing a good job. Term limits take power and responsibility away from the voters.

Just as term limits can prevent poor or unsuccessful presidents from remaining in office, so too can they force successful presidents out of office before people are ready to see their careers end. If presidents are doing a great job, why make them leave office after eight years? Shouldn't that decision be left to the people?

The White House

Conclusion

It's time to get rid of term limits!

Our country is a democracy. In a democracy, the people have the right to vote for whomever they want for president. The decision about whether a president stays or goes should be made by the American people as well, not by an amendment that was passed nearly 60 years ago. In times of crisis or hardship, many people would prefer to keep a president with the experience necessary to get the country through difficult times. That means having the option to keep a president in whom they have confidence for a third term. In addition, it's important for presidents to have enough time in office to make sure their new policies are up and running and helping those people they're intended to help. Getting rid of term limits would allow experienced, capable, intelligent, and popular presidents to remain in office for as long as the voters believe that they are the best people for the job.

Should There Be Presidential Term Limits?

NO!

incumbent

person who is currently holding an office

insider

person who has information or privileges that the average person does not

lame duck

an elected official still in office but not slated to continue

monarchy

nation governed by a king or queen

policy

a plan or course of action chosen to guide people in making decisions

term

the time for which something lasts, such as the time an elected official serves in office

Twenty-Second Amendment

law added to the Constitution stating that a president can be elected to office for only two terms

unbiased

not favoring one way of feeling over another

Glossary

abolish
to do away with

amendment
change or addition to the Constitution

bill
document that proposes either to change
the law or to make a new law

briefing
informational meeting

bureaucracy
people running government bureaus
or departments

campaign
series of activities aimed at winning
an election

candidate
person who runs for or is nominated for an office

Congress
lawmaking body of the United States government,
consisting of the Senate and the House of
Representatives

constituent
voter

Constitution, the
set of laws stating the fundamental principles
of our government

cronyism
appointing a friend to a position